SESAME STREET

SESAME STREET MECHA BUILDERS

I0869420

Plan It, Test It, Solve It

Solving Problems with the Sesame Street Mecha Builders

Nicole Gabor

Lerner Publications ◆ Minneapolis

Join the Mecha Builders on a learning adventure! In this book, young readers will discover how to plan it, test it, and solve it using critical-thinking skills. Children will be empowered to be creative problem solvers by asking questions, being curious about possible solutions, and persevering in the face of challenges.

Sincerely,
the Editors at Sesame Workshop

Table of Contents

You Can Solve Problems! 4

Use Problem-Solving Skills 6

Try It Out: Build Your Own Ramp 28

Glossary 30

Read More 31

Index 31

You Can Solve Problems!

You can learn problem-solving skills in everyday moments by exploring, investigating, and discovering. Let's learn how to solve problems with the Mecha Builders!

Use Problem-Solving Skills

The first step to solve a problem is to observe what the problem is. *Observe* means to use your senses, like sight, sound, and touch, to find out more about something.

After you observe, investigate how to solve the problem.

Investigate means to take a closer look at something to understand it better. You can say:

"I wonder . . ."

"What if . . . ?"

"Let's try . . ."

Asking questions can help you come up with a plan to solve the problem.

Next, try out your plan! If your first idea doesn't work, try another. Never give up—you can learn a lot from your mistakes!

The Mecha Builders solve problems by doing three things:

Plan It

They think of ways to solve the problem.

Test It

They try different ideas and don't give up.

Solve It

They find a solution.

You can try to solve problems just like the Mecha Builders!

Mechas, we have a problem to solve! Elmo wants the toy car to go from the starting line to the finish line, but the car is not moving.

Let's plan it!
Mecha Builders, gear up!

Elmo wonders if the toy car will cross the finish line if Elmo gives it a push. Let's try!

When Elmo pushed the toy car, it only went halfway to the finish line and then stopped. It didn't cross the finish line! How can we make it go farther?

Me have idea!
A ramp!

Great idea! A ramp might help get the toy car to the finish line. Ramps can help things get from high to low quicker and roll farther.

Elmo wonders if we should put the toy car at the top of the ramp. Maybe it will go farther than when we pushed it. Let's test it!

If your first idea doesn't work, try again!

This time, the toy car went farther than when Elmo pushed it, but it still didn't cross the finish line. I wonder if the ramp is too low.

What if we build a higher ramp? Elmo thinks that might help the toy car go farther.

Mechas, let's test it!

It worked!
We did it!

We solved the problem, Mechas! The toy car crossed the finish line!
Because the toy car started up higher, it was able to go quicker and roll farther.

At first, Elmo thought a push would get the toy car to the finish line.

Then, me thought ramp could help. But ramp too low.

Now we know that for the ramp to make the toy car reach the finish line, it needed to be higher at the top when the toy car started the race.

Next time you have a problem to solve, remember these steps from the Mecha Builders:

Think of ways to solve the problem.

Try different ideas and don't give up.

Find a solution and save the day!

Try It Out:
Build Your Own Ramp

You can build a ramp with things you have at home! Follow these steps:

1. Find something that's long and flat, like a picture book, a cutting board, or a board game box.

2. Lean one end of the long and flat item on top of something to make a ramp.

3. **Test it!** Send anything that rolls down the ramp. Try a toy car or truck, a ball, or something smooth.

4. **Ask questions!** What items move the quickest or the slowest? What other objects can you test?

5. **Keep exploring!** Make the ramp higher or lower and see what happens.

GLOSSARY

investigate: to take a closer look at something to understand it better

observe: to use your senses to learn about something

ramp: a platform or surface that goes from high to low or low to high

solution: an answer to a problem

READ MORE

Golkar, Golriz. *How to Problem Solve*. Blue Owl Books. 2026.

Krekelberg, Alyssa. *Finding Solutions: Problem Solving*. Child's World, 2021.

Peters, Katie. *Planning Ahead*. Lerner Publications, 2022.

INDEX

investigate, 8

mistakes, 10

observe, 6, 8

senses, 6

solution, 12, 27

PHOTO ACKNOWLEDGMENTS

Image credits: FatCamera/Getty Images, pp. 5, 7, 11, 13, 18; SolStock/Getty Images, pp. 9, 16; Maskot/Getty Images, p. 13; 020 Creative/Getty Images, pp. 21, 22; d3sign/Getty Images, p. 25. Design element: enjoynz/Getty Images.

For Sebastian, Christian, and Audrey

© 2026 Sesame Workshop. Sesame Street, Sesame Street Mecha Builders, and all related trademarks, characters, and design elements are owned by Sesame Workshop.

International copyright secured. No part of this book may be reproduced, stored in a retrieval system, or transmitted in any form or by any means—electronic, mechanical, photocopying, recording, or otherwise—without the prior written permission of Lerner Publishing Group, Inc., except for the inclusion of brief quotations in an acknowledged review.

Lerner Publications Company
An imprint of Lerner Publishing Group, Inc.
241 First Avenue North
Minneapolis, MN 55401 USA

For reading levels and more information, look up this title at www.lernerbooks.com.

Main body text set in Mikado.
Typeface provided by HVD Fonts.

Editor: Brianna Kaiser **Designer:** Viet Chu
Photo Editor: Lucien Brinkley
Lerner team: Martha Kranes

Library of Congress Cataloging-in-Publication Data

Names: Gabor, Nicole author
Title: Plan it, test it, solve it : solving problems with the Sesame Street Mecha Builders / Nicole Gabor.
Description: Minneapolis : Lerner Publications, [2026] | Includes bibliographical references and index. | Audience: Ages 4-8 | Audience: Grades K-1 | Summary: "Plan it, Test it, Solve it! When people use critical thinking skills, they can solve everyday problems. Young readers join the Mecha Builders in learning how to test and solve problems"— Provided by publisher.
Identifiers: LCCN 2025010826 (print) | LCCN 2025010827 (ebook) | ISBN 9798765685082 library binding | ISBN 9798348029029 paperback | ISBN 9798765697504 epub
Subjects: LCSH: Mecha builders (Television program)—Juvenile literature | Problem solving—Juvenile literature | Critical thinking—Juvenile literature
Classification: LCC BF449 .G33 2025 (print) | LCC BF449 (ebook) | DDC 153.4/3—dc23/eng/20250825

LC record available at https://lccn.loc.gov/2025010826
LC ebook record available at https://lccn.loc.gov/2025010827

Manufactured in the United States of America
1-1012833-54584-8/5/2025